LIFE AS I SEE IT

through poetry

Herbie Dunnan

authorHOUSE

AuthorHouse™ UK
1663 Liberty Drive
Bloomington, IN 47403 USA
www.authorhouse.co.uk
Phone: UK TFN: 0800 0148641 (Toll Free inside the UK)
UK Local: (02) 0369 56322 (+44 20 3695 6322 from outside the UK)

© 2024 Herbie Dunnan. All rights reserved.

No part of this book may be reproduced, stored in a retrieval system, or transmitted by any means without the written permission of the author.

Published by AuthorHouse 10/31/2024

ISBN: 979-8-8230-9055-1 (sc)
ISBN: 979-8-8230-9056-8 (e)

Library of Congress Control Number: 2024922895

Print information available on the last page.

Any people depicted in stock imagery provided by Getty Images are models, and such images are being used for illustrative purposes only. Certain stock imagery © Getty Images.

This book is printed on acid-free paper.

Because of the dynamic nature of the Internet, any web addresses or links contained in this book may have changed since publication and may no longer be valid. The views expressed in this work are solely those of the author and do not necessarily reflect the views of the publisher, and the publisher hereby disclaims any responsibility for them.

CONTENTS

My Friend 1
The Gym 3
Eat To Live Not To Die 4
Mental Health 5
The Florist 7
Tatoos 8
Plan B 9
Equally Equality 10
Dementia 11
Comfort Zone 13
My Friend [end of] 14
When I Die 15
Stay Away Father 16
Rambo Knife or Tongue 18
Interracial Love 19
Who Are You 21
Playing With Words 23
Our Inventions 25
Cut 26
Aphro-Disiac 28
My Ineyon 29
Vitamin D. 30

Waiting in Vain	31
I Wonder	32
Me Time	33
Culture Day in School	34
Flight Sergant; Peter Brown	36
Its Not Ok But Its Alright	37
The Table	38
The Streets	40
Poetry	41
Writing A Poem	42
BBB	43
Living Alone	45
Women of Wealth	46
Let's Do It	48
Early detection is protection	49
Well done	50
Racism in schools	51
They call it banter	52
My life-thank you	53
Acknowledgements	55
Dedications	57

MY FRIEND

I can't pick up the phone anymore to speak to my dear friend,
Her passing was an untimely end,
I can't pick up the phone to ask, miss; what's gwarning?
I still look at my phone and hope she will soon be calling.

The years we spent as colleagues and friends will never be erased.
A friend like her can never be replaced
Kind, sincere, loving and caring too
In my hearts of hearts, I will never forget you.

She told me at each stage what was going on
But she always seemed so positive and strong.
I never thought that it would come to this
But the hope I had never exist.

A week before she passed. She called me and said.
She said they had given her two weeks; I held my breath I couldn't speak.

When someone means the world to you
Its hard to say goodbye
You know you won't see them again
You just keep asking yourself why?

THE GYM

In the gym together we're training,
I hear no one speaking of race hate; or complaining,
Everyone is working out; all you hear is grunts and groans
Trying to make gains is their only moan.

In the gym everyone's united, hijab wearers,
And people with dreadlocks too
Seasoned trainers mixing with the new

No one cares how you look,
there are many different sizes,
There are big and small people
All working to their own devices.

EAT TO LIVE NOT TO DIE

Its essential to eat good food
Not to live long but to live healthy
To help you with your task
I must tell everybody.

Eat to live not to die, will help with your ambition
Seeking knowledge of what to eat?
They'll give you their opinion

They will open your ears and eyes
On healthy living,
Give thanks and praise to Ekong and his team
Nuff respect and blessings.

MENTAL HEALTH
[By Cinara Tugay]

Shouldn't this event not be every week?
I can't express the way I feel, when I try,
I end up feeling defeated and weak.

Suffering with manic depression and anxiety.
I couldn't see past twenty-one
I now know it can happen to anyone.

It's a terrible combination of a disorder, if it is not controlled
So, my advice to you; is don't let it get a hold,
Don't live trapped inside of a high, people love you
And don't want to give you an early goodbye.

Mental health caught me by surprise, I could say
I almost lost my life
I barely made it; but I'm glad that I survived.

Most people are addicted
to weed and booze, it seems now if I hadn't coped
The way I did
I don't think I would be writing this to you.

Mental health is everywhere; be safe and aware.
The person you're next to could be suffering
Ask them if they are, ok?
And show them that you care.

THE FLORIST

Flowers can't bring anyone back from the dead
But we make the florist rich,
time is the healer
But one day our clock will stop tick.

All I can say is wonder what is to become of you
RIEP is all I can say
Sleep well and God bless you.

TATOOS

You wear weave, lipstick and lashes, but when
You saw me you said woo!
You looked at me and said, that's evil,
Because I have got a tattoo.

But who is wrong and what is right?
Artistry on your body I think is a delight
You must also think that, or you wouldn't
Where does it say I shouldn't?

African tribes have done this for years,
To mark their culture, position, and fears.
I'm not going against, just doing my thing
So put me right if what I say is wrong, please tell me your position.

PLAN B

Some men don't realise that they are only plan B.
This only comes into contention because their woman was set free
He didn't want her so to save face,
She started dating you, yes, you've taken his place.

You asked her for a date before he came on the scene
You weren't her type then, she wasn't keen.
But you pursued her and waited for your chance
Now he's dumped her, she's back searching for romance.

Her heart is still with him, though she says its not
But now she's looking for anyone to fill his spot
So, plan A. deleted her, now she's back to you plan B.
You are the closest she can see.

EQUALLY EQUALITY

Why can't a woman pull out
the chair for a man?
Why does it have to be we?
Why can't a woman pay for the meal?
They want equality.

DEMENTIA

Mary's got dementia she was alright before
Some would say she's losing it
But she's fading more and more.
She used to be an elder, in her community
Now she sits alone looking out the window: dementia is her enemy.

Her children and grandchildren live far away
All she looks at through the window
Are children on the street at play
She once had a husband, but he passed some years ago
Now they have moved her far away
To a place that she doesn't know.

It's sad, when she was younger and had a lot of friends
Partying, shopping and eyeing up all the men.
But that was years gone by, now she's in a predicament

No more family to help her
The window is her friend.
Time goes by so fast. And no one really know
If they'll bypass dementia, because more and more it grows.

COMFORT ZONE

We all like our comfort zone, staying where we are
But by staying in your comfort zone, you won't get very far,
If you want to move up; then you must. leave people and things behind,
they may not want to grow, and it shows in their lack of trying.

We all like our comfort zone
Sticking to what we know,
But we can all do better
We've all got that get up and go.

MY FRIEND [END OF]

You're supposed to be my friend Well at least I thought you were
I thought we could speak to each other; but now our friendship is obscure.
You haven't spoken to me because of something that I said?
Well, if you can't tell me what it is this friendship is so dead

Friends are supposed to be honest and truthful,
Be able to speak their minds, not hide and hold what they want to say deep inside.
And if you don't like things I say speak your mind too
We're friends, tell me you don't like it; then I'll know what to do.

Well, I still hold you dear, my feelings are real
But I can't help the way that you feel
Life is too short for holding things within
Maybe I'm skating on thin ice and may just fall in.

WHEN I DIE

When I die, don't cry
You're crying for what reason?
When I die, please don't cry
I'm still here; I'm not leaving
When I die, please don't cry.
I beg you, stop grieving.
When I was alive you didn't want to know
So please stop deceiving.

STAY AWAY FATHER

I never wanted to be a stay away dad,
for me that post was created
your mum said that's what she wanted
it wasn't even negotiated

my hands tied, her family on her side
so, I walked away with damaged pride.
oh, I fought; and went to court
they gave me access of sorts.

It wasn't what I wanted. I wanted to be with you
Selfishness created this mess, I just had to pull through.
I didn't even get to know your teachers or any of your friends,
Did they know you had a real daddy? and not one that pretends.

Leaving school, you got your first job, which was very exciting
You moved on and had kids, to see them I wasn't even invited

You changed completely, not the loving child I once knew,
I'm left alone with just memories of you.

What she put in your head, now cannot be erased
It seems my once loving daughter's mind has now been replaced
You're older now, I thought that things would've Changed,
It seems she took control, and yet I get the blame.

RAMBO KNIFE OR TONGUE

They both cause severe damage
Rambo knife and tongue,
Both cause long lasting injuries
When all is said and done.

If you get cut with one
You can bleed to death
The other can be hurtful
Make you sit and fret.

Harmful and toxic both can worry you to death
Both are weapons of destruction,
Be careful how you set.

INTERRACIAL LOVE

It's not your fault you both fell in love
Though you're both from different races
It caused upheaval in your families
Wow! The look on their faces.

But for all you've been through
You stood by each other
Now both loving parents
Father and mother.

Some family members,
Thought it would never last
Your family said all this
Now it's all in the past.

With your lovely children times have not been easy
You've met challenges, upheaval and unrest.
You've prayed, and are now happy
Because your whole family's blessed.

You gave up your side of the family
In your love you wanted to invest
It's worked out well for you,
Your love has passed the test.
The pressures that a mixed-race couple go through
Only they alone can tell,
But by sticking by each other
You've now really excelled.

WHO ARE YOU

At home he's really smitten with his wife and kids
Not the same guy we know at work, our workmate Sid,
The king of the one liner and all his jokes are blue
I don't know which of him is true.

He buys the tabloid newspapers
I've heard at home; he reads the Times.
At work he freely talks about when he was young
And committing naughty crimes.

Apparently, he was popular with the girls
He's had five of a baker's dozen
He even told us of the time
He nearly dated his second cousin.

At home he is a different man
His family gets his full attention
He has a lovely house
Although it's not a mansion.

He doesn't go out much,
he loves spending time with the kids
He's a happy family man
Our cheeky workmate Sid.

PLAYING WITH WORDS

Eat good food, socialise and hydrate
Manicure, pedicure, exfoliate, concentrate
Delegate, but don't manipulate, don't frustrate,
Or exacerbate, take time to meditate in yourself feel great.

Eat good food, masticate, don't dwell or fixate
Speak clearly, don't abbreviate
Don't hide who you are accentuate
Stay calm, don't get irate, ask questions, investigate.

Slow down, don't accelerate,
don't expect it all on a plate
Work for what you want without debate
Pursue your goals don't abdicate.

Eat good food, stimulate your palate
If you can't be a friend then be a mate, just try to facilitate.

If you make love, be passionate, show you care be considerate.
Don't legislate, if you have no mandate,
Light up, illuminate. Turn on your inner switch, activate.

OUR INVENTIONS

We invented most things but got no credit,
I know they hate us, there; I said it.
No recognition, we signed it all over
We thought we were helping and doing them a favour.

It hurts to think that we were that naïve,
We thought they were helping us
But were deceived, sign on the dotted line then you can get your papers,
We thought yeh ok, no more slave masters.

But it wasn't so and to this day
They're still abusing us and feeling no way,
When we retaliate, they call us aggressive,
And try to make out we're all manic depressive.

But we continue to invent, and without consent
They still steal our dreams.
It's something they did before
Stealing our plans and schemes

CUT

As I walked into the room, I saw pills on the table
She was just lying there not willing or able,
I rushed to you; turned you on your side
To dislodge the pills from your throat and I cried.

It was then I saw the note that was crushed in your hand
I couldn't make head or tail; I couldn't understand.
I called the emergency services and tried to resuscitate.
But to no avail, when they arrived, I thought I'd failed.

They rushed to try to keep you alive,
the note in your hand was now on my mind
help her Lord pull her through,
I screamed out in horror, when they said; there's nothing they could do.

I tried to take the note from her hand, the police said no!

That's for us, understand? I fell to the floor and curled into a foetus,
The way I was feeling was now obvious,
the police came and asked,
What did I know? And did I touch the body? I said she was my girl you know.

I just came in and saw her there, what do you mean if I touched her?
Of course I shared.

When the director shouted CUT! I felt so elated
The scene stretched my skills; I felt exasperated.
To make this movie I went through hell,
Its now playing on my mind, but I'll try not to dwell.

APHRO-DISIAC

Her name says it all and she was no plane jane
Her beauty and elegance had brought her fame,
She would make Mr Freeze melt.
If you need to talk to her, then fasten your belt.

Men with a low libido are mentally cured
What she exudes you just can't ignore,
She's that kind of lady there's nothing that she lacks,
That's why they call her Aphro Disiac.

MY INEYON

I have a Ineyon in my life, I have known her for years.
We get on well; although we have shed tears,
I used to say my situationship, but that ship has now sailed
Not because of problems or because we've failed.

A Ineyon in Korea means providence of fate
It's a spiritual vibe to which we can relate
Its specifically about relationships; like you were meant to be
Whatever happens in your life; even living separately

A spiritual connection and it cannot be detached
It cannot be broken because you're spiritually matched.

VITAMIN D.

There's a lot of black people lacking vitamin D.
This is not my assumption.
it's what my doctor is telling me
the melanin that protects us from the sun
is also blocking our vitamin D absorption.
We might not be vulnerable to skin cancer
But in vitamin D we are lacking,
Thinking all is good without even knowing.

WAITING IN VAIN

You've been living a lie, it's time to wake up
He doesn't love you its time to face up,
He treats you well but that's not all that you want
You want him to love you, but he just can't.

He's not that type he doesn't show emotion
He can't give you love and devotion.
This is what he lacks it's in his genes
His dad was the same and never on the scene.

He's also been hurt before, and it made him cry
Swore it wouldn't happen again until the day he dies
He's a nice guy polite and has manners
But his whole life is in tatters.

So if love and devotion is your main,
Sorry you're just waiting in vain.

I WONDER

I wonder, if you ever wonder how your daddy is?
I wonder if you pray to God and ask him to forgive.
I wonder if you wonder how your dad is doing.
Are you happy with the fact of you not knowing?

I wonder if you remember when daddy used to give you hugs
Put his arms around you and show you all his love.
I wonder when there was lockdown; was he on your mind?
You had time to think then, your dad could have been dying.

I wonder if you'd be proud of your dad, and what he has achieved?
Working hard all his life by rolling up his sleeve,
Your dad is wondering what is going on.
He needs to know what he has done wrong.

ME TIME

I like a little me time its me and me alone
I cherish my me time that's why I live alone
Some say I'm selfish it's me, my myself and I,
I'm happy with myself; and here's the reason why.

I write poems and watch TV I can multitask
Do cooking and ironing, no one there to ask
I make my mind up for myself, no one doing it for me,
I go to the gym or walk around the park for free.

CULTURE DAY IN SCHOOL

It's nice to see the students supporting their countries
They're representing, from primary to secondary,
Members of staff they are also representing
Some wonder and try to guess; what country is that student wearing.

There's a sense of togetherness,
As students in their class are doing subjects
That are culturally biased.
The kitchen today have got their work cut out, cooking this and cooking that
From countries all about.

Rice and peas, chicken, fish and chips, if you please
Jollof rice and plantain, and macaroni cheese.
It's a lovely day and there is an array, of good food
But I hope we don't ever forget black history; that would be rude.

Black history year in year out
In lessons it must be taught
Least we forget the divisions
And the battles fought.

FLIGHT SERGANT; PETER BROWN

He left Jamaica years ago to fight for this country
He died alone in his flat, not knowing he had family.
It's all a shame and oh so strange; that it happened recently
Thinking, where was his friends and family?

It s sad that they had to put out a call
For people to attend his funeral,
But in the end, it was attended
by the military's high officials.

Flight sergeant Peter Brown
The black air man from Jamaica,
World war two pilot, who became
One of this country's saviours.

ITS NOT OK BUT ITS ALRIGHT

You say you don't love me, but I'm not putting up a fight
Its not ok but it's alright
You say you want to leave, well it's your right,
Its not ok but it's alright.

If that's your decision, I hope it makes your future bright
Its not ok but it's alright
If you want me back, ill be back to stay
Its alright and with that I'm ok.

THE TABLE

What are you bringing to the table?
You were once young willing and able
You set up your plan to grab a good man
Now you're acting like you're disabled

It takes two to tango so help him
Don't let him get hot up and sweltering,
He's done his bit now credit it,
It seems like you're not helping.

You're telling your friends; you chose the wrong guy
Now you run to them and cry,
Complaining he's this and he's that
And you don't know where the relationship is at.

It takes two in any relationship
he's stuck by you regardless
he brought it to the table when you were both willing and able
but now you're considering a split,

you wanted a good man, you set up your plan
mow you're talking negatively
like a poison chalice, you bear him malice
but the truth is clear to see.

THE STREETS

The streets are not paved with gold
They are littered with zombie knives
Young boys running around
Ruining each other's lives.

It's a sad situation, our young men facing extension
Trying to prove what? I don't know.
You say you got beef with guys on the streets
No respect for the streets do you show.

Another youth slain, another family in pain
When is it all going to end?
It's a sad situation we need elevation
We need to mix and blend.

POETRY

With poetry I express my thoughts and feelings
I can go deep, sometimes too revealing.
I can also impress which is stimulating
But it's not for everyone it can also be annoying.

When I start a poem im always anticipating,
When I finish a poem, the feeling is elevating
While writing a poem, I'm procrastinating
But I never give up, for me it's all accelerating.

WRITING A POEM

A poem can be written in a day, a week, or a year
You get an idea make a note, then you write and make it clear.
The idea and content are the main thing
I don't even worry about the spellings
That can be sorted out later, when you start editing.

Writing poems give me a buzz
And keeps my mind working
It is a great sense of achievement
That's why I love to keep on writing.

It means a lot to be able to put your thoughts on paper
The completion fills you with joy,
there's nothing greater.
You may also in the end like to find yourself a publisher.

BBB

Black boys, Black men, Black fathers
Don't let your life become a disaster
Teach each other to grow and rise
We should be helping each other.

Help each other to build and create businesses
We all need to survive
We need pluses not minuses
We need to stand up and survive.

We need to let our people grow
Why are we fighting each other?
Everyday it's the same thing
A brother disrespecting a brother.

We've fought against slavery
Some say we're still fighting
Yet we're killing our own
When we should all be uniting.

Black boys. Black men, black fathers
We need to help each other out

Stop destroying our people with knives
Greed and word of mouth.
Thinking you own the ends
You can't see the damage you're causing
Making demands of youngers,
Leading them to criminalising.

LIVING ALONE

Some people live alone and yes, they're happy
But sometimes its good to be checked on by somebody
People say they care but do they really?
You shouldn't have to prompt them, obviously.

They claim we're brothers, sisters
And the rest, but that don't cut it for me
That doesn't past my test.

Some people live alone by choice
But still need checking on; or to be given advice,
It's nice when someone calls, it shows that they care,
But some just don't bother, they're not sincere.

WOMEN OF WEALTH

You're all amazing, and you're working it well
And the reason why you are here
Is because you are ambitious as well.

Beautiful as you all are what gets a real man going
Is a woman with a positive mind
And someone that is knowing

Some women think that they're not worth it
So straight away they give in
But if you are positive and strong
The chances are you'll win.

You all have a lot to offer and I'm sure that you'll grow
Ask the questions you need to ask
That's the only way you'll know.

So, ladies I say to you open and shine
Because each of you are worth it
Singularly. You are one of a kind.

Love is an addiction when its good you want more
Being successful is also an addiction
And something you all adore.
If you put your mind to it you will all conquer
The more you'll succeed
Getting stronger and stronger.

People will look at you and wonder how you did it
But they didn't see the work you put in
And the times you nearly blew it.

LET'S DO IT

Sisters always say; they're doing it for themselves
It's time we men got together instead of sitting on the shelf
Time to pick each other's mind
And find out what we're all thinking.

EARLY DETECTION IS PROTECTION

Early detection is protection
We may not know we cannot tell
But it effects one in two women
And one in eight men.

We don't know if we don't know when
So, men encourage your women,
Women encourage your men.

Statistics show that if caught early
You have more of a chance,
There's no need to be afraid or embarrassed,
So go to your doctor; demand a check
This thing call cancer we must intercept.

Some get it more than once
They get treatment, but still, it advance
Some get it and are in remission
A cancer free world is everyone's vision.

WELL DONE

Narcotics and drinks were his downfall
But my friend you conquered them all Twenty years now; you've been free I'm so proud of you, wow!

We met in college, and I remember us talking
As we trained, how time have passed, and you've grown
Let's enjoy what you've done

Here's to another twenty years; my friend
I'll be eighty-six then, and hope you post and
Let us know that you've done it once again.

RACISM IN SCHOOLS

It's not in schools it needs to be tackled
It needs to be tackled from home
It's been going on for years
But will it ever be done?

Racism is hurtful, it can turn your inside out
It's not just someone shouting the
N word,
It's the slight negative comments I'm talking about.

In the recent riots, there were kids there brought by mum and dad
shouting racist comments, how sad.
We can teach why it's wrong in schools

But we need to find the core, Or it will just go on, and on
And develops more and more.

Racists will tell you they're not racist
It proves they don't understand,
They need educating, spreading hate all over the land.

THEY CALL IT BANTER

They call it banter, and use it as their mantra, But to us it's still an isim,
No matter what they call it, We still call it; Racism.

MY LIFE-THANK YOU

Thank you for the Life that you've given me Lord
I really can't complain,
Though I'm unlucky in love and my body aches
I really can't complain.

Thank you, Lord, for giving me so much; I have more than many,
But I'm aware, there's some that don't have any.
Sometimes I forget to say thank you daily,
But you're forever in my mind even when I don't express it.

Our country is not embroiled in war, earthquake, floods or total devastation,
but still mankind has been
destroying the world your wonderful creation

I have friends and family; people to talk to when it matters,
Some families are not close, so the relationship shatters.

But thank you for the life that you've given me, you know I say this from the heart. You're always by my side, you've been there from the start.

In God I trust

ACKNOWLEDGEMENTS

I would like to thank the library
staff at Oasis academy hadley
For introducing me to the school,
putting my work on display.
Forever promoting me and giving
me advice, Chloe Lebow
And Fadime Ozbek.
Also, Rakin Fetuga, your general support
and meaningful talks are uplifting,
I listen and hear you.
Helen Octhere, my dear friend, from
our talks about writing and publishing
books it has come to this.
Finally, Cinara Tugay, thank you
for allowing me to include
Your heart felt poem MENTAL
HEALTH the first time I heard it I was
blown away and wanted to include it,
you are a talented young woman.
You see it and say it like it is.

I thank you all

DEDICATIONS

This book is dedicated to my dear
friend, colleague, motivator and rock
Who sadly went to sleep on the 28/03/2024
She was an inspiration to me and
still reigns supreme in my life
Gone from this world but not from my heart
Rest In Eternal Peace
Gabriella Medina Noa 1984-2024

Printed in Dunstable, United Kingdom